KNOW HOW KNOW WHY

WONDERS
OF THE WORLD

Written by Colin Dibben

Illustrations by Phil Gleaves/SpecsArt

TOP THAT

Licensed exclusively to Top That Publishing Ltd
Tide Mill Way, Woodbridge, Suffolk, IP12 1AP, UK
www.topthatpublishing.com
Copyright © 2014 Tide Mill Media

THE PYRAMIDS OF GIZA

The Great Pyramid of Khufu, or Cheops, was the tallest structure on Earth for 43 centuries. It is both the oldest and the best preserved wonder of the ancient world.

What are the pyramids of Giza

Giza •
Cairo •

EGYPT

Pyramids are found in Egypt.

The pyramids contain the tombs of ancient Egyptian kings or pharaohs. There are three large pyramids at Giza, a 'necropolis' or city of the dead, outside Cairo. The largest and oldest is the Great Pyramid of Khufu, or Cheops, which was once 145.75 m (481 ft) high. Nearby are the Pyramids of Khefre and Menkaure and the famous Sphinx statue.

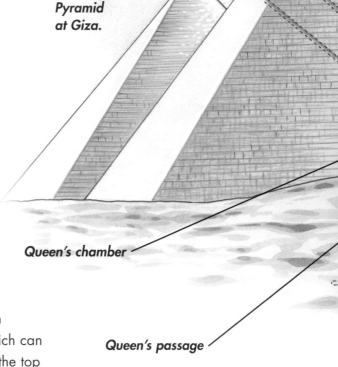

The Great Pyramid at Giza.

Queen's chamber

Queen's passage

How was the Great Pyramid built

The Great Pyramid took twenty years to build during Pharaoh Khufu's reign, around 2560 BC. Thousands of slaves carved and carried two million stone blocks, each weighing over 1,814 kg (2 tons). Ramps were used to drag the blocks into place. The pyramid was covered in smooth stone – bits of which can still be seen near the top of Khefre's pyramid.

Slaves hauling large stone blocks.

What is the significance of the shape of the pyramids

The pyramids have a very geometrical shape. The ancient Egyptians thought that using fixed shapes like the square, the circle and the triangle in their buildings would allow their civilisation to survive floods and droughts. They thought that the shape of the pyramid, reaching out to the stars, would bring the pharaoh closer to the gods and make him live forever.

What is the Sphinx

The magical statue of the Sphinx at Giza has a lion's body and the face of Pharaoh Khefre. It is 73.5 m (241 ft) long and 20 m (65 ft) high. The Sphinx was carved out of solid rock around the time of the construction of the Pyramid of Khefre in 2555–2532 BC.

The Sphinx at Giza.

King's burial chamber

Grand gallery

Unfinished chamber

FACT BYTES

Westminster Cathedral and St Paul's cathedral in London, St Peter's in Rome, and the cathedrals of Florence and Milan would all fit inside the Great Pyramid!

FACT BYTES

The pyramids are so old that an ancient Arab proverb says: 'Man fears Time, yet Time fears the Pyramids'.

What is inside the Great Pyramid

Mysterious corridors and galleries lead to Khufu's burial chamber at the heart of the pyramid. The pyramid was so well designed that there is only 1 cm (one third of an inch) between the tomb and the chamber walls. The galleries once contained beautiful precious objects, but over the years thieves have stolen everything. Khufu's servants may have been sacrificed inside the pyramid.

THE STATUE OF ZEUS AT OLYMPIA

To bring the god of thunderbolts to life and celebrate the Olympic Games, the most famous ancient Greek sculptor created an enormous golden statue.

What were the ancient Olympic Games

The ancient Olympic Games were held near Athens.

In Greek legend, gods and goddesses came from a mountain outside Olympia, 70 km (43 miles) from Athens. Every year from 776 BC to AD 391, wars stopped all over the Greek world and athletes came to Olympia for competitive games in honour of Zeus, 'the father of gods and men'.

Entrance to the original Olympic stadium, Olympia.

Who was Zeus

Zeus lived on mountain tops and in clouds, where he kept an eye on the other Olympian gods and naughty humans, too. Although he was the most important god, Zeus often had to zap other Olympians with thunderbolts to keep them in order. The Olympians were definitely not 'one big, happy family': Zeus's father Kronos ate his own children!

The impressive Statue of Zeus at Olympia.

When was the Statue of Zeus built

In 430 BC, the sculptor Pheidias finished a terrifying 13-m (42-ft) statue. The height of a four-storey building, the statue barely fitted into the Temple of Zeus. Visitors had the statue's feet at eye level. Zeus was seated but looked as though he was about to explode out of the temple. His flesh was ivory, his drapery gold, and his throne was decorated with precious stones.

FACT BYTES

The Statue of Zeus held a figure of the winged goddess of victory in one hand. Her name was Nike, which is where the sports brand name comes from!

FACT BYTES

Pheidias also made the marble sculptures on the Parthenon in Athens. These are known as the Elgin Marbles and can today be seen in the British Museum in London.

How was the Statue built

Pheidias built a wooden frame on which sheets of metal and ivory were placed. He sculpted and carved the different pieces of the statue in a workshop before assembling them in the temple. As the statue was designed to be out of proportion to the temple, it looked bigger than it was. For almost four hundred years, it fascinated everyone who saw it.

What happened to the Statue of Zeus

The Olympic Games were outlawed in AD 391 by the Christian Emperor Theodosius I. The temple was closed and then badly damaged by earthquakes, landslides and floods. In the fifth century AD, the ruined statue was taken to a palace in Constantinople, where it was unfortunately destroyed by fire in AD 462.

The ruined Temple of Zeus.

THE HANGING GARDENS OF BABYLON

The massive walled city of Babylon was full of wonders, but none could match the Hanging Gardens, the greatest example of hydraulic engineering in the ancient world.

Babylon, on the River Euphrates.

Where was Babylon ❓

Babylon was built on the banks of the River Euphrates in Iraq. This area is called 'the cradle of civilisation', because the world's first cities were constructed there. Babylon had massive walls, one hundred bronze gates and brightly tiled buildings full of golden statues of the god Marduk. The 91-m (300-ft), multi-coloured Tower of Babel stood at the city's heart.

Who built the Hanging Gardens ❓

In 570 BC, King Nebuchadnezzar II built an enormous terraced garden next to his palace, to please his wife Amyitis. Nebuchadnezzar was a great military commander, and was very proud of making Babylon the most beautiful city in the world. Bricks in Babylon bore the inscription 'Nebuchadnezzar made this'.

King Nebuchadnezzar.

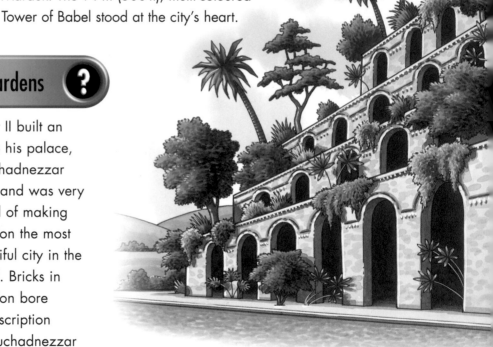

The beautiful Hanging Gardens at Babylon.

FACT BYTES

The ancient historian Herodotus believed that when Babylonians died they were buried in honey. Sweet, but definitely untrue!

Why were the Hanging Gardens so special ❓

The Hanging Gardens were built on an 24-m (80-ft) high, man-made hill. The hilltop was packed with beautiful and exotic trees and flowers. The hill was actually a series of terraces – also full of flowers and plants – supported by strong pillars. Ingenious machines called chain pumps helped to irrigate the garden. Although the gardens didn't really 'hang' the name probably came from a Greek word meaning 'overhanging' and they must have been an impressive sight with their beautiful plants overhanging terraces and arches.

Why might the Hanging Gardens be a myth

As Babylonian records make no mention of the Hanging Gardens, they may have been a myth. However, archaeologists have discovered possible evidence of garden cellars and chain pumps. The River Euphrates would have provided the water needed for the plants which would have been transported in buckets on the chain pump.

The Hanging Gardens were irrigated with water from the River Euphrates.

How did chain pumps work

Two wheels, one above the other, were connected by a chain, on which buckets were hung. When slaves turned the lower wheel, the buckets dipped into the River Euphrates and picked up water. The chain then lifted the buckets to the upper wheel, where they fed water channels running down through the Gardens.

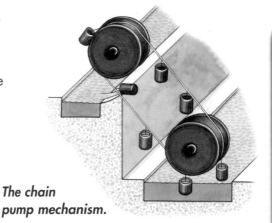

The chain pump mechanism.

What happened to the Gardens

The Hanging Gardens were first described when the warrior-king Alexander the Great invaded in 331 BC. By the time of the Persian invasion in the second century BC, the Hanging Gardens had disappeared, along with the city of Babylon.

Alexander the Great.

FACT BYTES

Babylon got all its food from the nearby Plain of Edin, which is the Bible's Garden of Eden

THE TEMPLE OF ARTEMIS

Antipater of Sidon, the man who listed the Seven Wonders of the World in the second century BC, thought that this was the best of them all!

Why was the Temple so impressive

The Temple of Artemis is at Ephesus.

The Temple of Artemis at Ephesus – on Turkey's Mediterranean coast – was built in about 550 BC. It was enormous and made out of marble. The Temple was 80 m (260 ft) wide, 130 m (420 ft) long and had 127 18-m (60-ft) high columns. The overall height of the Temple was 24 m (80 ft). The Temple housed four huge bronze statues of warrior women or Amazons.

The Temple of Artemis.

Who was Artemis

Artemis was the Greek goddess of hunting and fertility. According to legend, she was friendly to humans, especially children, and also protected animals. At night, she was supposed to dance through the countryside, firing arrows of moonlight from a silver bow. Artemis was still very popular in the early days of Christianity.

Statue of the Greek goddess Artemis.

Who was Herostratus

In 356 BC, a man in Ephesus called Herostratus was obsessed with becoming famous. He burned down the Temple of Artemis so that everyone would talk about him, but the authorities made it illegal to say his name! The Temple burned down on the night that Alexander the Great was born. Legend says that Artemis was too busy at the birth to save her own temple.

FACT BYTES

In ancient times, the number seven was thought to be the purest of numbers – which is why Antipater of Sidon included only seven wonders on his list!

When was the Temple rebuilt

When Alexander the Great conquered Asia Minor, he helped rebuild the Temple, which was finished by 335 BC. In AD 262, Goths destroyed the Temple, but Artemis was still so popular that the Ephesians vowed to rebuild it. For some reason, they never did.

The ruins of the Temple of Artemis.

Why did the Temple become an important Christian site

St Paul preached in the Temple in the first century AD and was almost attacked by the angry worshippers of Artemis. Legend has it that the Virgin Mary, accompanied by St Paul, came to Ephesus at the end of her life, sometime between AD 37 and AD 45. St John is said to have lived the last years of his life nearby.

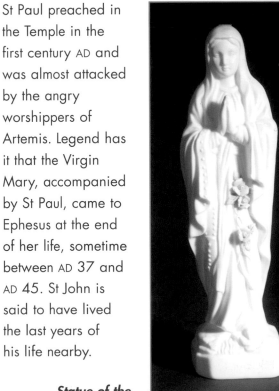

Statue of the Virgin Mary.

FACT BYTES

Some of the remains of the Temple of Artemis can be seen in the Ephesus Museum, Turkey and the British Museum, London.

Marble statues, Ephesus Museum, Seljuk, Turkey.

THE TEMPLE OF ARTEMIS

THE MAUSOLEUM OF HALICARNASSUS

The world's first great memorial monument was packed with statues of lions, horses and people – all the things that Satrap Mausolus loved in life.

The port of Halicarnassus is now known as Bodrum.

What does the word 'mausoleum' mean ?

The word 'mausoleum' means a large, stately tomb. The history of the word dates back to 350 BC, when a magnificent tomb was built for Mausolus, the ruler of Halicarnassus, a large port on the Aegean Sea in south-west Turkey. Mausolus's 'mausoleum' was planned by his wife, Artemisia.

What is a satrap ?

Mausolus was a satrap, or local governor, for the mighty Persian Empire. In the century before the Mausoleum was built, the Persian Empire spread from Iran into Iraq, Northern India, Syria, Egypt and Turkey. The empire was so big, local rulers were used to help control people. Mausolus's province of Caria was almost 1,600 km (1,000 miles) from the Persian capital of Persepolis.

A figure of Mausolus.

Who were the Amazons ?

The Mausoleum of Halicarnassus was decorated with a frieze depicting fighting Amazons – bits can be seen today in the British Museum in

The ornate frieze depicting fighting Amazons.

London. In legend, the Amazons were warrior women who fought Greek heroes. The Amazon queens Hippolyte, Penthesilea and Antiope were very strong and very beautiful. Female societies really did exist in Ukraine and Libya – and evidence suggests that they were great horsewomen and fearless fighters.

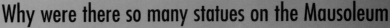

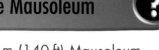

FACT BYTES

The proper word for a stone tomb is a 'sarcophagus', which is ancient Greek for 'flesh eater'!

You can still see the foundations of the Mausoleum if you visit Bodrum in Turkey.

Why were there so many statues on the Mausoleum ?

The 45-m (140-ft) Mausoleum was famous for its statues of people and animals. The tomb stood on a podium covered with statues – the roof was teeming with them and a huge statue of a chariot pulled by four horses adorned the top. It was the first ancient building dedicated to the memory of a human being rather than a god.

The remains of a colossal horse from the quadriga of the Mausoleum at Halicarnassus.

Why was the Mausoleum destroyed ?

In AD 1494, Crusader soldiers called the Knights of St John of Malta decided to fortify a nearby castle with stones from the Mausoleum. By AD 1522, the whole Mausoleum had been taken to pieces and used. The massive Crusader castle still stands at Bodrum, and the polished stone and marble blocks from the Mausoleum can be seen within the walls.

The Mausoleum of Halicarnassus.

Crusader castle at Bodrum.

THE MAUSOLEUM OF HALICARNASSUS

THE COLOSSUS OF RHODES

This enormous, polished bronze statue shone like the sun for only 56 years, but it became a powerful symbol of unity for all Greek people.

The Greek island of Rhodes housed the Colossus.

Why was the Colossus built

Ancient Greece was made up of city-states that often fought each other. On the island of Rhodes there were three such states, but, in 408 BC, they united. One hundred years later, to celebrate a unity that was now the envy of all Greece, the people of Rhodes built an enormous statue to their sun god, Helios. The Colossus was finished in 282 BC.

Where did the Colossus stand

For a long time it was thought that the Colossus straddled the mouth of the main harbour in Rhodes, but, given the great height of the statue and the width of the harbour mouth, this is impossible. Recent research suggests that the Colossus was actually erected on the eastern side of the harbour.

Rhodes harbour today.

How was the Colossus constructed

The bronze skin was made in pieces in the workshop of a local sculptor, Chares. The feet and ankles were fixed to a white marble base and the skin slowly attached to an iron and stone frame. An earth ramp was used to work on the top. When the Colossus was finished, it was 33 m (110 ft) high.

The iron and stone frame of the Colossus.

How was the statue paid for

Rhodes traded a lot with Egypt. In 305 BC, King Seleucus I of Macedonia besieged the island in an attempt to break this trade link between Rhodes and his enemy, Ptolemy I of Egypt. Seleucus's army eventually sailed away, leaving behind their military equipment. The people of Rhodes sold this and used the money to build the Colossus.

When was the Colossus destroyed

The statue stood at the harbour entrance until an earthquake in 226 BC broke its knees and the Colossus fell over. The Egyptians offered to restore the statue, but an oracle forbade it. For nearly 900 years the Colossus lay in ruins, until AD 654, when the remains were sold to a Syrian merchant. Nine hundred camels were used to take the fragments away!

The statue destroyed.

The Colossus of Rhodes.

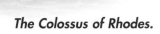

FACT BYTES

The Statue of Liberty in the harbour at New York was inspired by what the sculptor, Auguste Bartholdi, heard about the Colossus of Rhodes.

After the Colossus had fallen over, people used to try to reach around its left thumb and touch the fingers!

THE LIGHTHOUSE OF ALEXANDRIA

Sailors appreciated this lighthouse because it protected them. Builders stood in awe because it was then the tallest structure on Earth. Scientists wondered how the mysterious mirror worked!

Where was Alexandria

The city of Alexandria is in Egypt.

Alexander the Great built an empire stretching from Greece to Persia, Egypt and Asia Minor. He founded a city in Egypt, on the Mediterranean coast, and called it Alexandria. After his death in 323 BC, the empire split. Ptolemy I assumed power in Egypt and made Alexandria the greatest city in the world. Seleucos I of Macedonia ruled the empire from Greece to Babylon.

Why did Alexandria need a lighthouse

Alexandria was the greatest port on the Mediterranean Sea, but its double harbour made sailing dangerous. Luckily, the coastline around Alexandria was very flat so building a lighthouse to warn ships was not difficult. When the Lighthouse was completed, it was the tallest building on Earth!

FACT BYTES

The French, Italian, and Spanish words for 'lighthouse' come from the name of the island on which the lighthouse stood, Pharos.

The Lighthouse of Alexandria.

Who built the Lighthouse of Alexandria

The building of the Lighthouse on Pharos, an island in Alexandria's harbour, took twenty years and was completed in 270 BC. The finest

scientists, mathematicians and artists of the age planned the structure and its mirror in the famous Alexandria Library. The Lighthouse was 117 m (384 ft) high – the equivalent of a modern-day, 40-storey building.

The Alexandria Lighthouse compared to a modern multi-storeyed building.

How bright was the light reflected from the Lighthouse

According to historians, the huge mirror at the top of the Lighthouse was so well made, the light it reflected could be seen 50 km (35 miles) away. Apparently, the reflection was so intense it could burn up enemy ships! The mirror reflected sunlight during the day and a fire set in front of it at night. It was probably lifted into place using the internal shaft of the structure, which was also used to lift the fuel for the fire.

The intense light reflected from the Lighthouse.

What happened to the Lighthouse

The Lighthouse of Alexandria remained in use for almost fourteen centuries, until it was damaged by earthquakes in AD 1303 and AD 1323. The Egyptian Sultan, Qaitbay, used blocks from the Lighthouse to build a massive fortification in AD 1480. Recently, divers discovered the remains of the Lighthouse in the harbour at Alexandria.

The harbour at Alexandria today.

FACT BYTES

The Lighthouse of Alexandria was so famous, it still appeared on Roman coins hundreds of years after it was built.

THE GRAND CANYON

Discover how the most spectacular canyon in the world was made – and how you could be walking on the bottom of an ancient sea bed if you go there!

How big is the Grand Canyon

Grand Canyon

• Colorado Plateau

ARIZONA

The Grand Canyon cuts through the Colorado Plateau in Arizona.

The awesome Grand Canyon cuts through the Colorado Plateau in the American state of Arizona. It is 466 km (290 miles) long, 16 km (10 miles) wide and 1.6 km (1 mile) deep. The Colorado River runs through the Canyon, roaring over 200 rapids and dropping 670 m (2,200 ft) as it makes its way to the Gulf of California.

Aerial view of the Colorado River.

How was the Grand Canyon made

The Grand Canyon is the most spectacular example of 'erosion' in the world. The Colorado Plateau was created by violent movements on Earth's surface two billion years ago. The Grand Canyon has been carved by the movement of the Colorado River over this plateau during the last six million years.

The eroded rocks that form the Grand Canyon.

Why are there fossils at the top of the canyon

Visitors to the top of the canyon are walking on the bottom of an ancient sea bed – that is why you can find fossils there! Five hundred million years ago, the whole plateau was under water. When sea creatures died, the minerals in the sea turned them into fossils. Then the plateau was pushed out of the sea by massive explosions.

A fossilised trilobite found in the Grand Canyon.

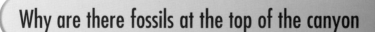

John Wesley Powell.

Who discovered the Grand Canyon

The first European to see the Canyon was a Spanish conquistador, Garcia Lopez de Cardenas in 1540. From the top, the river was so far away that he mistook it for a stream – and then wondered why it took three days to get there! In 1869, American John Wesley Powell took a boat down the entire length of the Canyon – a dangerous trip that took three months.

Why has the Grand Canyon changed in recent years

Over 2,000 species used to live in the Canyon. The ecology of the area depends on floods, but a dam, opened in 1963, now regulates the river. The damage caused by floods has been immense – much more than that caused by five million tourists every year and pollution from nearby cities and power plants.

An aerial view of the Grand Canyon.

The craggy and rocky terrain of the Grand Canyon.

FACT BYTES

In walking from the rim of the Grand Canyon down to the river, you pass through as many ecological zones as if you had travelled from Canada to Mexico!

THE NORTHERN LIGHTS

At the northern reaches of our planet, the raging sun and Earth's magnetic fields create the ultimate light show!

What are the Northern Lights

The Northern Lights.

The Northern Lights, or aurora borealis, form a 3,218-km (2,000-mile) wide oval above the Earth's magnetic north pole. At night, the Lights start as a faint glow on the horizon. Slowly, they turn into an astonishing green, red, pink, blue and violet curtain of light that curves and bends across the sky.

Where else do auroras happen

The Southern Lights, or aurora australis, occur over Earth's Southern Hemisphere. The Southern and Northern Lights are connected by Earth's magnetic field. Their displays are symmetrical, which means that the shape of the Northern Lights is a mirror image of the Southern Lights. The planets Saturn, Jupiter and Uranus also have colourful auroras over their magnetic poles.

Auroras occur at the Poles.

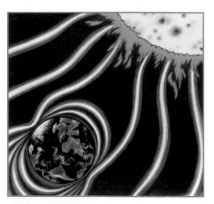

Solar winds.

How are auroras caused

Auroras are caused by the sun, which shoots a stream of matter and energy into space. When this stream, called a solar wind, reaches Earth it smashes into Earth's magnetic field. Particles from the stream spiral down towards Earth's magnetic poles. When they encounter Earth's atmosphere, these particles react with oxygen and nitrogen to make colourful swirls in the sky.

What did ancient peoples think the lights were

In Scandinavia, where the lights are really spectacular, people thought they were dragons battling in the sky. Inuits believed that the lights were torches held by the dead, showing the dying how to get to heaven. More recently, the lights were thought to be reflections of the dawn, the sun or the moon on ice in the atmosphere.

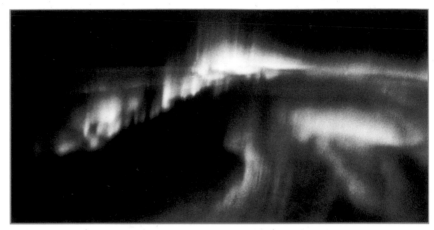

Inuits believed that the lights were torches held by the dead.

The stunning sight of the 'aurora borealis'.

Where do you go to see an aurora

In the Northern Hemisphere, the best place to see auroras is outside Fairbanks in Alaska. In the Southern Hemisphere, the best place is off the coast of Antarctica. During violent solar winds, Earth's magnetic poles shift. Then the aurora slips towards the equator, giving sky-gazers as far south as Mexico a real treat!

FACT BYTES

Earth is like a huge magnet that is surrounded by a magnetic field that can attract or repel things. Earth also has 'poles', or places where its magnetic power is concentrated.

The coast of Antarctica is the best place to see auroras in the Southern Hemisphere.

THE NORTHERN LIGHTS

THE VOLCANO OF PARICUTIN

There are active volcanoes all over the world, but only once have people seen a terrifying volcano born right in front of them.

Who saw the Volcano first

Paricutin in Mexico – site of the volcano.

On 20th February, 1943, a farmer named Dionisio Pulido was working on his land in Paricutin, a Mexican village. Suddenly, the ground opened up and a cone of earth rose with a thunderous noise, spewing out hot ash. Within a day, the cone had grown 45 m (150 ft) and was shooting rocks 304 m (1,000 ft) into the air.

How much damage did the Volcano of Paricutin do

Church spires stick out of the lava field left by the Volcano of Paricutin.

Molten matter called 'lava' poured out of the volcano and swallowed up two villages – you can still see the church spires sticking out of the lava field. The lava flowed for nine years, eventually covering 25 sq km (10 sq miles). Luckily, only three people died – they were struck by lightning caused by the eruption.

What makes a volcanic eruption occur

About 95 km (60 miles) under our feet there is a layer of very hot rock that sometimes melts, producing a molten liquid called 'magma'.

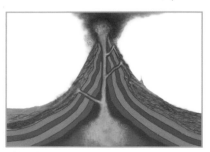

A volcanic eruption.

Pressure pushes magma towards Earth's surface, where it can 'erupt', which means explode violently, through the ground. Magma changes into lava – which is much thicker than magma – and ashes when it is exposed to Earth's atmosphere.

Why is Paricutin so important ?

Erupting volcanoes had usually existed for thousands of years but, before Paricutin, scientists had never witnessed the actual birth of a volcano. Scientists solved many mysteries surrounding volcanoes by studying Paricutin – such as exactly how magma behaves just before it breaks through Earth's surface.

Where can an active volcano be seen ?

Mount Etna, in Sicily, is a good place to go. In 2002 and 2003, Etna was the site of one of the most spectacular eruptions of the last four centuries. Some 30 million cubic metres of lava and 40 million cubic metres of rock and ash were produced. Other very active volcanoes include Kilauea in Hawaii and Nyamuragira in Africa.

Mount Etna is an active volcano in Sicily.

FACT BYTES

The cone shape of a volcano is made from the ashes and rock that shoot out of it and then compact when they fall back down to the ground.

FACT BYTES

The Volcano of Paricutin grew to a height of 335 m (1,100 ft) in just one year and its ash fell on Mexico City, over 321 km (200 miles) away!

A Mexican flag in front of the National Cathedral, Mexico City.

The Volcano of Paricutin.

MOUNT EVEREST

Thousands of brave men and women have accepted the ultimate challenge – to climb as high as you can go on Earth and look down from the top of the world!

Where is Mount Everest

Mount Everest is on the borders of Nepal and Tibet.

Mount Everest is the highest mountain in the world. It is part of the Himalayan range on the borders of Nepal and Tibet. Mount Everest towers above the other mountains at 8,848 m (29,029 ft) high. The summit of Mount Everest is as high as you can go on Earth – it really is the top of the world!

How was Mount Everest formed

Roughly 55 million years ago, India, which was then a separate continent on its own tectonic plate,

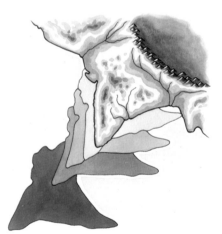

Indian and Asian plates collide.

began to move. Eventually, it collided with the 'plate' of Asia, and the coasts where the two continents met were pushed up – a bit like the bonnet of a car in a crash. These coasts became the highest mountain range in the world.

Why is it called Mount Everest

Westerners call it Mount Everest, but the Tibetans call it Chomolungma and the Nepalese call it Sagarmatha – and they should know, because they live at the mountain's base. First recognised as the highest mountain in the world in 1852, it got its Western name ten years later, when Sir George Everest, a British surveyor, came to the area.

Tibetan mother and child.

Who were the first men to climb Mount Everest

Climbing Mount Everest has been the ultimate challenge for climbers ever since the 1920s. Climbers have to contend with a lack of oxygen and bitterly cold temperatures. New Zealander Edmund Hillary and his Nepalese guide Sherpa Tenzing Norgay were the first men to successfully reach the summit, on 29th May, 1953.

Mount Everest in the Himalayas.

Sherpa Tenzing Norgay (left) and Edmund Hillary (right).

Who else has climbed Everest

Since 1953, around 4,000 climbers have reached the summit. They have been as young as thirteen and as mature as 76. Junko Tabei became the first woman to reach the top in 1975. The fastest descent came in 1988, when Jean-Marc Boivin paraglided off the summit and reached the base in eleven minutes. Davo Karnicar skied down the mountain in 1980!

FACT BYTES

The tectonic plates of India and Asia are still pushing up against each other. As a result of this, Mount Everest grows by around 5 cm (2 in.) every year.

Mount Everest, Tibet.

Jean-Marc Boivin paraglided off Mount Everest.

MOUNT EVEREST

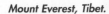

THE COLOSSEUM IN ROME

The design of most modern sports stadiums is based on this truly colossal ancient monument – one of the most famous archaeological wonders of the world.

How big was the Colosseum

Rome, where the Colosseum ruins can still be found.

Until the nineteenth century, the Colosseum in Rome was the largest amphitheatre in the world. It was 50 m (165 ft) high, 185 m (600 ft) long and large enough to hold 50,000 spectators. The façade, or exterior, was three 'arcades' – sets of 80 arches – on top of each other. Canvas material was hung from the fourth storey to protect spectators from the sun.

Why is the Colosseum's design so clever

The 'elliptical' Colosseum.

The Colosseum's design is full of 'elliptical', or squashed circle, shapes, which allowed more people to fit in. Behind the outer arcades, two corridors circle the building, with two smaller circular corridors inside them. The elliptical arena was surrounded by a wall to protect spectators from wild animals used in the games.

FACT BYTES

The Colosseum had 76 vomitoria, which sounds like the sort of place you go to if the games get gruesome. In fact, the word simply means gate!

Who built the Colosseum

The Emperor Vespasian began construction in AD 72. His son Titus held the first games there in AD 80, but the building was actually completed by Vespasian's younger son, Domitian, in AD 81. The structure was originally called the Flavian Amphitheatre because all three of these emperors came from a family called Flavius.

Emperor Vespasian.

What games were played there ❓

The most popular games were bloody contests between gladiators, or between gladiators and animals. Athletics, battle re-enactments and pageants also took place there. Some people think that lions ate Christians in the arena, but this is untrue. Gladiator combat was abolished in AD 404, and the last animal fight was held in AD 523.

The Colosseum in Rome.

A gladiator fighting a tiger.

FACT BYTES

In films, you often see the Roman Emperor give the 'thumbs down' sign when he wants someone killed by a gladiator. In fact, 'thumbs up' meant 'kill him' and 'thumbs down' meant 'spare him'.

What is the Colosseum like today ❓

Fires, earthquakes and neglect have badly damaged the Colosseum since it was last renovated in the early sixth century. However, over one-third of the outer arcades remain and the inner supports for the cavea, or seating space, are also visible. It is in remarkable condition when you consider that it was built nearly 2,000 years ago.

The Colosseum as it looks today.

THE GREAT WALL OF CHINA

The largest built structure in the world snakes across deserts, grasslands and mountains – and over two thousand years of history.

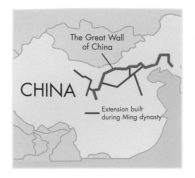

How long was the Great Wall of China ❓

The Great Wall once stretched 6,400 km (4,000 miles) from the Korean Peninsula to North-Central China. The Wall had an average height of 10 m (32 ft) and was 5 m (16 ft) wide. Its 'snake' shape is due to the fact that it follows the course of the rivers and the contours of the mountains and valleys around it.

Who built the Great Wall ❓

In the seventh and eighth centuries BC, Chinese rulers built walls to protect their communities. The first emperor, Qin, joined all of these walls together between 221 and 206 BC. Over the next century, the Han emperors extended the Great Wall across the Gobi Desert. The Great Wall was at its longest during the Ming Dynasty of AD 1368 to 1644.

Qin Shi Huang, 1st emperor of China.

FACT BYTES

Ordinary people were forced to build the Great Wall. So many of them died that it is sometimes called the 'longest cemetery on Earth'.

Why was the Great Wall built ❓

Ancient China was plagued by attacks from Mongolian and Manchu people. Emperor Qin wanted to build a massive fortification that would stop these raiders from the North. In later centuries, the Great Wall was used to transport soldiers. It was also used to transmit messages across the empire. This was done by burning fires on the watch towers and sending smoke signals.

How was the Great Wall built ?

The early Great Wall was made of earth. During the Ming Dynasty, brick and stone were used to build walls, watch towers and garrison posts. In many areas, there were no farms or towns to provide food, so the workers and the soldiers depended on dangerous mountain supply routes. Many of the builders died.

One of the Great Wall's towers.

What state is the Great Wall in ?

The Great Wall worked for centuries, but after the Manchu seized China in 1644, it fell into disrepair. Even now there are no Chinese laws protecting the Great Wall, although it was made a UNESCO World Heritage Site in 1987. Several hundred kilometres of the Great Wall remain in Eastern China.

The Great Wall of China as it stands today.

The Great Wall of China stretched 6,400 km (4,000 miles).

FACT BYTES

Some people think that the Great Wall can be seen from space. It can only be seen from a low orbit – as with so many other buildings.

The Great Wall of China seen from a low orbit, TERRA Satellite.

THE TAJ MAHAL

One of the most beautiful buildings in the world, the Taj Mahal was built as a monument to love – but it ended up ruining a mighty emperor.

Who were the Mughals

The Mughals were fantastically rich Muslim emperors who ruled Northern India from the sixteenth to the nineteenth century AD.

The Mughal Empire (red).

They were descended from fearsome Turkish and Mongolian warriors, and early emperors like Akbar, Jehangir and Shahjehan waged war to amass their fortune. The Mughal capital was at Agra, about 200 km (124 miles) south of New Delhi.

Who was the Taj Mahal built for

The Mughal Emperor Shahjehan ordered the building of the Taj in 1631, after the death of his wife, Mumtaz Mahal, in childbirth. Shahjehan wanted

Emperor Shahjehan.

his wife's tomb to be the most beautiful building in the world. Construction began in 1631 and was completed in 1653. Masons, craftsmen, sculptors, and calligraphers came from all over Asia to work on the masterpiece.

Why is the Taj Mahal so beautiful

The Taj is probably the most beautifully proportioned and symmetrical building in the world. It is set in a garden of fountains and ornamental trees. The decoration is very extravagant – some small decorations have fifty gemstones in them. The minarets, or praying towers, have been cleverly designed to make the building look bigger than it really is.

What is strange about the colour of the Taj Mahal

Emperor Shahjehan was so rich that he built the Taj almost completely out of marble. When light strikes the marble at different times of the day or night, it produces different soft colours or hues. In full moonlight, the Taj glows white, at sunrise

The silhouette of the Taj Mahal at dusk.

it looks pink and at sunset it looks gold. Visitors say the effect is very beautiful – and very sad.

What happened to Shahjehan

It took 22 years and 22,000 workers to complete the Taj Mahal. Shahjehan's memorial was so expensive to build that he had no money left when it was finished. His son deposed him and threw him into prison. From his prison cell Shahjehan could gaze at his wife's tomb through a window.

FACT BYTES

When the Taj Mahal was finished, Shahjehan cut his workers' hands off so they couldn't make anything as beautiful ever again.

The famous Indian poet Rabindranath Tagore called the Taj Mahal 'a teardrop on the cheek of time'.

The Taj Mahal, Agra, India.

THE TAJ MAHAL

MACHU PICCHU

The lost city of the Inca sits on a remote mountain top in Peru. For nearly four hundred years it lay hidden, with only the roaring river in the valley below to keep it company.

Who were the Inca

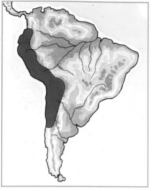

The Inca Empire (red).

The Inca Empire was the largest empire in the Americas. It stretched 4,828 km (3,000 miles) from Ecuador to Chile in South America, and had 13 million subjects. The supreme ruler was called the 'Inca'. The Inca Empire started around AD 1450 and was already ruined by civil war when Spanish invaders arrived in AD 1532.

When was Machu Picchu discovered

The Spanish didn't believe rumours about a hidden Inca fortress high in the Andes mountains. In 1911, an American, Hiram Bingham, climbed up through a rain forest 193 km (120 miles) from the Inca capital of Cuzco to behold the ruins of a small city. He was the first person to see the city for almost 400 years.

What was Machu Picchu

Machu Picchu (left) is built on terraces on a 2,761-m (9,060-ft) mountain top. It may have been a fortress, a religious centre or a royal retreat. Bordered on three sides by precipitous river canyon walls and invisible from below, the people fed themselves by cultivating agricultural terraces. The city had 150 houses, temples and baths.

FACT BYTES

The building blocks at Machu Picchu weigh 45,350 kg (50 tons) each but fit together so precisely you can't slip a knife blade between them.

What is the Intihuatana stone ?

There is an observatory at Machu Picchu. Inside it is an Intihuatana stone – which means 'Hitching Post of the Sun' in Quechua, the Inca language.

At midday on 21st March and 21st September the sun appears directly above this stone and casts no shadow. The Inca believed that at these times they could influence the world around them.

The Intihuatana stone.

Why was Machu Picchu abandoned ?

Built in the 1450s, Machu Picchu was mysteriously abandoned just before the Spanish took the Inca capital of Cuzco in 1533. This is probably because the civil war weakened supply lines linking Inca cities, and life at Machu Picchu became too hard. In 1983, UNESCO named Machu Picchu a World Heritage Site and around 650,000 people visit the lost city of the Inca every year.

FACT BYTES

In modern-day Machu Picchu, llamas are used to keep the grass short!

The impressive city of Machu Picchu.

MACHU PICCHU

TEOTIHUACAN

In the history of mankind, there is only one ancient city that lives up to its name. Teotihuacan really is mysterious and grand enough to be the home of the gods.

Where is Teotihuacan

Teotihuacan was just north of where Mexico city is today.

The city of Teotihuacan was founded 50 km (31 miles) north-east of modern-day Mexico City sometime between AD 100 and AD 200. By the fourth century it was the sixth largest city in the world, stretching for 20 sq km (7 sq miles) and with 200,000 inhabitants. The city was mysteriously burned down and abandoned in AD 750.

Who built Teotihuacan

No one knows who built Teotihuacan or lived there. It was named Teotihuacan, which means 'the city where the gods were born', by people

Ylaloc, the rain god.

called the Aztecs – 500 years after it was abandoned! The Aztecs believed that only people who were as powerful as gods could have created such enormous pyramids and temples.

What can you see at Teotihuacan

The Pyramid of the Sun is arguably the largest pyramid in the world. It is 63 m (207 ft) high and is built over a sacred cave. This pyramid is connected to the Pyramid of the Moon by the 2.5-km (1^1/$_2$-mile) Avenue of the Dead. You can also see the amazing Temple of Quetzalcoatl, which is decorated with enormous stone snake heads.

Why is the design of Teotihuacan special

Teotihuacan was the first city in the Americas and its grid structure is still used 1,800 years later! The plan of Teotihuacan is very symmetrical: avenues point north, south, east and west, and the pyramids are modelled on sacred mountains surrounding the city. The city plan resembles butterfly wings – an insect that was sacred to the god Quetzalcoatl.

FACT BYTES

The Great Pyramid at Giza is taller than the Pyramid of the Sun but not as large. Another contestant for the world's largest pyramid is the Hotel Luxor in Las Vegas, USA (right).

Who was Quetzalcoatl

Quetzalcoatl was the name of both a god and a legendary hero. The god Quetzalcoatl is the god of food, rebirth, butterflies and serpents. He travelled all over Central and South America founding new civilisations. The Aztecs believed that Quetzalcoatl would return at the end of time, which was why they allowed the Spanish conquistadors to destroy them in 1519.

FACT BYTES

Twice a year the sun sets directly opposite the Pyramid and in a direct line of sight from a long tunnel referred to by archaeologists as 'a volcano tube'.

The Pyramid of the Sun at Teotihuacan.

A statue at the temple of Quetzalcoatl.

TEOTIHUACAN

THE MAASAI MARA

In some of the most stunning scenery in the whole of Africa, you can come face to face with the world's wildest animals!

Where is the Maasai Mara

The Maasai Mara is the most spectacular game reserve in the world. Located south of Kenya's capital, Nairobi, the Maasai Mara is part of the great Serengeti plain. It is over 1,510 sq km (583 sq miles) of rolling grassland, rocky outcrops and winding rivers – and boasts one of the highest concentrations of animals and animal species in the world.

Why is the Maasai Mara home to so many animals

The region is both humid and fertile. It is crossed by the rivers Mara and Telek, which are full of water all year long. This is unusual in Africa. The river banks are

Zebras on the Maasai Mara.

covered in thick bush and lush grassland. The abundance of water and food means there are almost always lions, leopards, cheetahs, elephants, buffalos, zebras, rhinos and hippos to see.

When is the wildebeest migration

Migrating wildebeest.

Each year, in August and September, millions of animals called wildebeest head to Mara from Serengeti, in search of better grass. This is one of the natural wonders of the world, as the wildebeests move across the plains in 44-km (27-mile) long columns. Predators like lions, leopards, cheetah and hyenas follow the columns, looking for easy prey.

What is a kopje ❓

The rolling plains of the Maasai Mara are pitted with rocky outcrops called kopjes. These rocks are millions of years old and home to lions, cheetahs, antelope, mongoose and large Verraux eagles. The kopjes are often decorated with ancient rock paintings, depicting life on the plains. These paintings are made by Maasai tribespeople.

A big cat in the wild.

FACT BYTES

Many people confuse cheetahs (top) and leopards (bottom). The main differences are that a cheetah looks smaller and has a dark 'tear mark' running from its eyes to its cheeks.

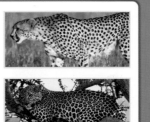

Who are the Maasai ❓

The Maasai are a famous warrior tribe whose lives centre on the herding of cattle. They live in small settlements called kraals, each of which is made up of

A Maasai tribesman with his cattle.

between eight and fifteen huts. The kraals are surrounded by a thornbush fence that is sharper than barbed wire. At night, the cattle and other domestic animals are brought inside the kraal for protection.

The Maasai Mara in Africa is teeming with wildlife.

FACT BYTES

The Maasai get their animal protein without killing their cows: they cut a cow's neck, collect some blood and drink it with milk.

THE MAASAI MARA

35

THE PETRONAS TOWERS

Over the last hundred years or so, people have been trying to construct the tallest building in the world. 'Skyscrapers' like these are symbols of pride – but they never hold on to the record for long!

How tall are the Petronas Towers

Kuala Lumpur, Malaysia.

The Petronas Towers in Kuala Lumpur, the capital of Malaysia, are 452 m (1,483 ft) tall. This made them the tallest building in the world at the time of completion. Each of the twin towers has 88 stories, a tapering point and a 74-m (242-ft) spire that brought it to its record-breaking height.

When were the Towers built

The architect, Cesar Pelli (right).

In 1991, there was an international competition to find a design for the headquarters of the government-owned oil company, Petronas. Architect Cesar Pelli won the competition and building started in 1994. The Petronas Towers cost about $1.6 billion to construct, and opened on 28th August, 1999. The double structure contains a concert hall, a library and an art gallery – as well as offices.

Why were the Towers built

Skyscrapers are usually built for the 'prestige', or honour, they bring their creators. The Petronas Towers were supposed to be a symbol of Malaysia's spectacular economic growth in the 1980s and early 1990s. Many of the Towers' design features also celebrate Malaysia's Muslim culture. Unfortunately, a worldwide recession started as building work on the Towers began.

Kek Lok Si Temple, Penang, Malaysia (Malaysian temple).

What is currently the world's tallest building

In January 2010, the Burj Khalifa in Dubai, UAE, opened and was declared the tallest building in the world. It reaches 829.84 m (2,723 ft) tall. The Shanghai World Financial Center still holds the record for the world's highest public observation deck at 474.2 m (1,556 ft). The observation deck in the Burj Khalifa is at 452 m (1,483 ft).

The Burj Khalifa, Dubai, is the world's tallest building.

Why are the Towers an architectural marvel ?

The Petronas Towers have an 'arabesque' design and the floor plans are based on the Islamic star. These geometric shapes allow for lots of office space – and great views! The towers are linked by a 'skybridge' on the 42nd floor. The exterior is made from ribbons of glass and steel that shimmer in the sun.

The skybridge link.

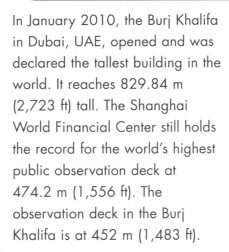

The Petronas Towers.

FACT BYTES

The Petronas Towers have about 32,000 windows. It takes window cleaners a month to clean each tower.

The CN Tower in Toronto, Canada is 553 m (1,815 ft) tall and was the tallest structure between 1976 and 2007.

THE PANAMA CANAL

For centuries, trading nations dreamed of connecting the two great oceans of the world. When they did, it was one of the greatest engineering feats of all time.

What is the Panama Canal

The Panama Canal links two oceans.

The Panama Canal is an 80-km (50-mile) waterway through Panama, linking the Atlantic and the Pacific Oceans. Before the canal, ships coming from Europe or the east coast of America travelled 20,900 km (12,958 miles) around South America to get to the west coast. The canal shortened voyages between New York and San Francisco to 8,370 km (5,189 miles).

Who built the Panama Canal

Charles I Spain.

In 1534, Charles I of Spain ordered a canal route through the Isthmus of Panama. The French worked on a canal from 1880 to 1900, but disease and financial problems defeated them. In 1903, the US began constructing the canal that is still in use today. Completed in 1914, it cost $375 million!

Why was the Canal such a feat

Excavation to build the Canal.

More than 56,000 people worked for ten years, excavating and dynamiting their way through hard bedrock. They cut through jungles, hills and swamps, and had to deal with tropical diseases like malaria and yellow fever. Engineering feats included building the biggest canal locks in the world and erecting a dam that provided enough power to run the Canal.

Why does a canal need locks

Waterways contain height gains called elevations that stop boats from continuing upstream. Canals have an ingenious way of moving boats to, or from, this higher water. Locks use the force of gravity on water to raise and lower boats. In the Panama Canal, one boat uses 52 million gallons of water to move through the Canal's three locks.

Large ships can navigate the Canal.

How do canal locks work

A lock has gates at either end. When a ship moves into the lock, the gates close and water is drained out (or pumped in, if the ship wants to go upstream). Due to gravity, the lock's water eventually equals the height of the water downstream or upstream. The gates at the front of the boat are opened and the ship goes on its way.

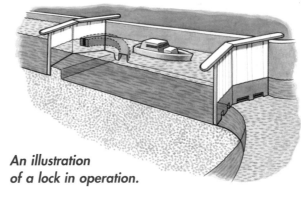

An illustration of a lock in operation.

The remarkable engineering feat of the Panama Canal.

FACT BYTES

On 4th September, 2011, the one millionth ship used the canal. The ships are guided by slow-moving, high-powered trains called 'mules'. As the ships proceed, mules move along each side to guide them in a straight line through the open lock gates.

THE PANAMA CANAL

THE ITAIPU DAM

Find out how a curtain of concrete 196 m (643 ft) high can turn one of the world's greatest rivers into energy and became the world's most powerful dam.

Where is the Itaipu Dam

The Itaipu Dam spans the Parana River on the borders of Brazil and Paraguay in South America. It is an 8-km (5-mile) wide dam, spillway and hydroelectric power plant. The dam is as high as a 65-storey building. It was built between 1975 and 1991 and supplies around 17 per cent of Brazil's energy and 73 per cent of Paraguay's.

How does a dam work ?

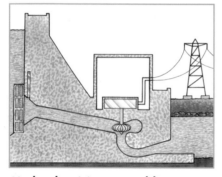

Hydroelectricity created by water.

A dam is a wall built across a river to block the flow of the river. The water builds up behind the dam in a reservoir. Pipes take water from the reservoir to cities, to irrigation projects, or to hydroelectric power stations, as at Itaipu. Here the water passes over turbines – huge wheels attached to motors – to create electricity.

What is a spillway

A dam's spillway.

The pressure of the water behind a dam can damage its structure, so every dam has a spillway. This works just like the overflow of a bath. When the water reaches a certain level, usually during floods, it flows down the spillway and back into the river below the dam. Itaipu's spillway can discharge 62,200 cubic metres of water per second.

How powerful is the Itaipu Dam

Itaipu's powerhouse, where electricity is created, contains twenty hydroelectric generators. Each turbine has enough power to supply electricity to a city of 1.5 million people. The turbines generate 14,000 MW (megawatts) of electricity. The highest electricity production was 94,684,781 megawatts-hour (MWh) in 2008.

Why do dams affect the environment ?

The creation of a reservoir means flooding the area behind the dam, which can destroy the delicate balance of an area's ecology. When Egypt's Aswan Dam was made, the builders had to move lots of ancient monuments. The Chinese government had to re-house over one million people when they built the Three Gorges Dam.

The Aswan Dam.

The Itaipu Dam.

FACT BYTES

Other famous dams include the Hoover Dam in America (right), the Aswan Dam in Egypt and the Three Gorges Dam in China.

THE EMPIRE STATE BUILDING

The most famous skyscraper in the world was the tallest building for over forty years. It remains the standard against which all other skyscrapers are judged.

What was the skyscraper race

The skyscraper race began with the Eiffel Tower (299 m/ 984 ft), in Paris in 1889. American architects, competing among themselves, started to build ever-taller buildings: the Metropolitan Life Tower of 1909 (213 m /700 ft); the Woolworth Building of 1913 (241 m/792 ft); 1929's Bank of Manhattan Building (282 m/927 ft); and the Chrysler Building in 1930 (318 m/1,046 ft).

The towers involved in the skyscraper race.

The Empire State Building.

When was the Empire State Building built

Construction began in March 1930 and was completed just one year and 45 days later, in May 1931. The Empire State Building is 381 m (1,250 ft) high and remained the tallest building in the world until the completion of the World Trade Center in 1972. It cost $40 million dollars to build.

The Empire State Building.

How was the Empire State Building built so fast

Workers known as skywalkers put up the immense frame, weighing over 50,000 tonnes in just 23 weeks. Passers-by would gaze up at them as they worked hundreds of feet above the ground, walking along the girders they put in place the day before to hammer big nails called rivets into steel girders higher up the structure.

A 'skywalker' at work.

Why was the Empire State Building built

In the early 1930s, the skyscraper was going to be an airport for dirigibles (also known as zeppelins or blimps) which were to be moored on the 102nd floor observation deck. The Observation Lounge that you can still visit on the 86th floor was going to be the departure lounge.

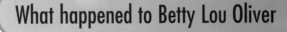

An airship, or dirigible.

What happened to Betty Lou Oliver ?

On 28th July, 1945, Betty Lou Oliver was working as a lift attendant in the Empire State Building, when a B-25 bomber crashed into it. Rescuers decided to lower Betty Lou in the lift, unaware that the cables were weakened. She rocketed over 300 m (1,000 ft) down the shaft in just seven seconds. The lift ended up in a cellar, but luckily Betty Lou survived.

The damaged building after the plane crash.

FACT BYTES

In 2003, Paul Crake set the record for the annual Empire State Building Run Up, climbing the 1576 steps to the 86th floor observation deck in 9 minutes 33 seconds.

Using the lifts, it is possible to travel to the 80th floor of the Empire State Building in 45 seconds.

THE EMPIRE STATE BUILDING

THE GOLDEN GATE BRIDGE

People said this magnificent bridge couldn't be built, but over sixty years after its completion, the Golden Gate Bridge remains the world's tallest suspension bridge.

What is a suspension bridge

Head on view of suspension bridge.

A suspension bridge has a deck (the bit pedestrians and motorists use) that is suspended from cables. The cables pass over towers and are secured in the earth. Bridges are subject to compression, a force that pushes down on the deck. The cables transfer this force to the towers from where it runs into the earth. Another force, called tension, affects the cables, but they are made taut and safe by the weight of the bridge.

How big is the Golden Gate Bridge

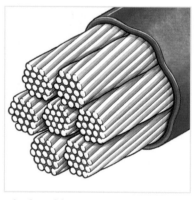

Thick cables support the bridge.

The bridge spans 2,737 m (8,981 ft) and can sway up to 8.2 m (27 ft) to withstand 160 km/h (100 mph) winds. The two towers are 227 m (746 ft) high and the cables – the biggest ever to support a bridge – are 110 m (361 ft) thick. Work on the bridge began on 5th January 1933, ended on 27th May, 1937, and cost $35 million.

Why is the Golden Gate Bridge painted orange

A paint was needed that would withstand the harsh winds, bad weather and corrosive salt air of the San Francisco Bay area. After tests, the choices were black, grey or orange. The architect thought darker colours would detract from the beautiful setting – and that orange could be seen better in dense fog. The colour used is called International Orange.

Why is it called the Golden Gate Bridge

?

In 1847, thousands of people came to San Francisco to look for gold in the Californian Gold Rush. The entrance to San Francisco Bay became known as the Golden Strait (or narrow channel). The Golden Gate Bridge spans this strait and was named after it.

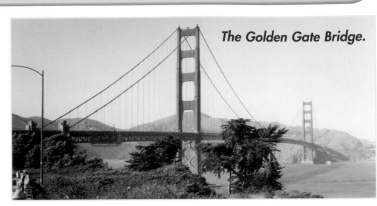

The Golden Gate Bridge.

Why was it thought impossible to build

The Golden Gate Bridge was considered impossible to build because of the fog, winds and ocean currents in the Bay. Workers wore goggles, hand cream and face cream – and a safety net was strung under the Bridge to protect them. They were also given special food so they wouldn't get dizzy!

A brave worker paints the Bridge.

FACT BYTES

The construction of the Golden Gate Bridge was the first time protective hard hats were worn on building sites.

The Golden Gate Bridge contains enough cable to go around Earth three times!

The world's tallest suspension bridge.

THE GOLDEN GATE BRIDGE

GLOSSARY

Agra
A city in north India and capital of the Mogul empire until 1658.

Alexandria
The chief port of Egypt on the Nile Delta: cultural centre of ancient times, founded by Alexander the Great.

Amazons
One of a race of women warriors of Scythia near the Black Sea.

Artemis
An ancient Greek goddess who was the twin sister of Apollo.

Asia Minor
The historical name for Anatolia (the Asian part of Turkey).

Auroras
An atmospheric phenomenon consisting of bands, curtains, or streamers of light, that move across the sky. As in aurora borealis (Northern Lights) and aurora australis (Southern Lights).

Babylon
The chief city of the ancient Mesopotamia. Home of the Hanging Gardens of Babylon.

Canyon
A gorge or ravine, especially in North America, usually formed by a river.

Chomolungma
The Tibetan name for Mount Everest, the highest mountain in the world.

Colosseum
An amphitheatre in Rome built around AD 75–80.

Colossus
A structure that's very large, such as a statue.

Conquistador
An adventurer or conqueror, especially one of the Spanish conquerors of the New World in the 16th century.

Crusader
European Christians who fought with Muslims to capture the Holy Land.

Cuzco
A city in south-central Peru: former capital of the Inca Empire, with extensive Inca remains.

Dam
A barrier of concrete, earth etc, built across a river to create a contained body of water.

Dirigible
Another name for an airship or a blimp.

Ecology
The study of the relationships between living organisms and their environment.

Emperor
A male monarch who rules or reigns over an empire.

Erosion
The wearing away of rocks and soil, etc, by the action of water, wind, ice etc.

Giza (El Giza)
A city in north-east Egypt, on the west bank of the Nile opposite Cairo.

Gladiator
A man trained to fight in arenas to provide entertainment.

Gold Rush
Started in 1848. More than 90,000 people made their way to California in the two years following James Marshall's discovery, and more than 300,000 by 1854.

Goth
A member of the East Germanic people from Scandinavia who settled south of the Baltic early in the first millennium.

Halicarnassus
A major Greek colony of the south coast of Asia Minor.

Helios
The ancient Greek god of the sun, who drove his chariot daily across the sky.

Hippolyte
A queen of the Amazons, slain by Hercules in a battle for her belt.

Inca
A member of the South American Indian people whose empire, centred on Peru, lasted from about AD 1100 to the Spanish Conquest in the early 1530s.

Kopje
A small, isolated hill.

Khufu
An ancient Egyptian king who was buried in the Great Pyramid.

Lava
Lava flowing from a volcano.

Magma
The molten liquid that results when a layer of very hot rock under the ground melts.

Machu Picchu
A ruined Inca city in South central Peru.

Manchu
A person from Manchuria, north-east China.

Maasai
A member of a Nilotic people, formerly noted as warriors, living chiefly in Kenya and Tanzania.

Mausoleum
A large, stately tomb.

Ming Dynasty
The Imperial Dynasty of China from 1368 to 1644.

Mongolian
An inhabitant of Mongolia, central Asia.

Muslim
A follower of the religion of Islam.

Olympians
Of, or relating to, Mount Olympus or the classical Greek gods.

Paricutin
A volcano in west central Mexico, in Michoacan state, formed in 1943 after a week of Earth tremors.

Pharaoh
The title of the ancient Egyptian kings.

Pharos
Any marine lighthouse or beacon.

Plateau
A wide, mainly flat area of elevated land.

Pyramid
A huge masonry construction that has a square base and four sloping, triangular sides.

Rhodes
A Greek Island in the south-east Aegean Sea, about 16 km (10 miles) off the Turkish coast.

Roman
Of, or relating to, Rome or its inhabitants in ancient or modern times.

Satrap
A governor in ancient Persia.

Serengeti
A park that covers 14,763 sq km (5,700 sq miles) of rolling plains in the African country of Tanzania.

Sidon
The chief city of ancient Phoenicia founded in the third millennium BC.

Skyscraper
A very tall multi-storey building.

Solar
Of, or relating to, the sun.

Summit
The highest part of a mountain.

Taj Mahal
A marble mausoleum in central India, in Agra: built (1632–53) by the emperor Shahjehan in memory of his wife.

Tectonic Plates
These are the results of the distortion of Earth's crust due to forces within it.

Trilobite
An extinct type of marine creature.

UNESCO
United Nations Educational, Scientific, and Cultural Organisation.

Vomitoria
A passageway that opens to a tier of seats.

Zeus
The supreme god of the ancient Greeks. The ruler of gods and men.

GLOSSARY

INDEX

Alexander the Great 7,8,9,14
Alexandria 14
Amazons 8, 10
amphitheatre 24
Ancient Greece 12–13
Artemis 8
Artemisia 10
Aswan Dam 41
aurora australis 18
aurora borealis 18–19
Avenue of the Dead 32
Aztecs 32

Babylon, gardens of 6–7
Bartholdi, Auguste 13
Bingham, Hiram 30
Boivin, Jean-Marc 23

Chares 12
Charles I of Spain 38
CN Tower, Toronto 37
Colosseum, Rome 24–25
Colossus of Rhodes 12–13

de Cardenas, Garcia Lopez 17
Domitian, Emperor 24

Egypt 2, 13, 14, 41
Elgin Marbles 5
Empire State Building, the 42–43

Ephesus, Turkey 8
erosion 16
Euphrates, River 6

fossils 16

gladiators 25
Golden Gate Bridge, the 44–45
Grand Canyon, the 16–17
Great Wall of China, the 26–27

Halicarnassus 10
Hillary, Edmund 23
Himalayas 22–23
Hoover Dam 41

Incas, lost city 30–31
Itaipu Dam, the 40–41

Karnicar, Davo 23
Knights of St John of Malta 11

lava 20
Lighthouse of Alexandria 14–15
locks 38

Maasai Mara, the 34–35
Machu Picchu 30–31
magma 20–21

Mara, River 34
marble 5, 8, 11, 12, 29
Mausoleum of Halicarnassus 10–11
Mausolus, Satrap 10
Mexico 20–21 32–33
Mount Etna, Sicily 21
Mount Everest 22–23
Mumtaz Mahal 28

Nebuchadnezzar II 6
Norgay, Sherpa Tenzing 23
Northern Lights, the 18–19

Olympic Games 4

Panama Canal, the 38–39
Parthenon, the 5
Pelli, Cesar 36
Petronas Towers, the 36–37
Powell, John Wesley 17
Ptolemy I 13, 14
Pulido, Dionisio 20
Pyramid of the Moon 32
Pyramid of the Sun 32
Pyramids of Giza 2–4, 33

Qaitbay, Sultan 15
Qin, Emperor 26

Rhodes 12–13
Sarcophagus 11
Sears Tower, the 37
Seleucus I 13
Serengeti Plain 34
Shahjehan, emperor 28
skyscrapers 36, 42
solar wind 18
Southern Lights, the 18
Sphinx 2–3
Statue of Liberty 13
Statue of Zeus 4–5
suspension bridge 44–45

Tabei, Junko 23
Taj Mahal, the 28–29
tectonic plates 22–23
Temple of Artemis 8–9
Temple of Quetzalcoatl 32–33
Teotihuacan 32–33
Three Gorges Dam 41
Tower of Babel 6

UNESCO 27, 31

Vespasian, Emperor 24
Volcano of Paricutin 20–21

World Trade Center, the 42

Zeus 4–5